C000181649

FOUNDATIONS
UNCOVERED

FOUNDATIONS UNCOVERED

Other foundation can no man lay
than that is laid, which is Jesus Christ
I Corinthians 3:11

THE APOSTOLIC FOUNDATION
OF THE
CHRISTIAN CHURCH

Volume One

JOHN METCALFE

THE PUBLISHING TRUST
Church Road, Tylers Green, Penn, Buckinghamshire.

Printed and Published by
John Metcalfe Publishing Trust
Church Road, Tylers Green
Penn, Buckinghamshire

—

© John Metcalfe Publishing Trust 1993
All Rights Reserved

—

First published September 1973
Second impression January 1983
Third impression May 1993

—

ISBN 0 9506366 5 7

—

Price 75p

—

CONTENTS

FOUNDATIONS UNCOVERED

I

The Fact of the Foundation

THE apostle Paul informs us in the first letter to the Corinthian church that 'Other foundation can no man lay than that is laid.'

And if laid, then the place of God's foundation—quite apart from the foundation itself—had been chosen already: in rock, not sand; of the Spirit, not the flesh; in the holy mountains of an eternal election, not the degenerate softness of a withered human will; on this rock of spiritual revelation, not that miry clay of fleshly works!

1

'Upon this rock I will build my church', Matthew 16:18, and at Corinth, by the apostle Paul, Christ built it, thus demonstrating further that the foundation of the Christian church had itself already been laid at the time at which the epistle was written, and fully laid at that. Others might build, but could not lay. The perimeter, area of building, was plainly marked out by previously sunk foundations, plain to discern for all future builders, and that solely in the rock of God's choosing.

Not only is it true that no other foundation of whatever sort is to be countenanced while time shall last, but moreover any other devised or imagined foundation than that already described in holy scripture is positively unlawful: 'can no man lay'! It is prohibited. Therefore all other vain religious excavations are of necessity laid in sand—itself unstable and impermanent—and shall prove in and of themselves unable to bear the strains and stresses later to be imposed upon them.

But the apostolic foundation once laid, is laid to take the weight of time and eternity, of an exceeding weight of glory, of the city of God. Divinely laid, laid in rock, laid in the holy mountains, that which the apostles founded is certain and secure and durable world without end. It is upon such a foundation and in such rock that Christ builds his church, and the gates of hell cannot prevail against it.

Moreover in the same passage the apostle Paul informs us, 'As a wise master-builder, I have laid the foundation'. That is, as an architect—*architekton*—he laid this foundation. Therefore, as one that designs. God has by the apostles rendered the design as well as the structure of the foundations of the Christian faith. And being a moral and spiritual foundation, it takes the form of sound words, of clearly defined truth; the true belief of which can bear the weight of eternity, and is that apostolic doctrine upon which the soul can rest safely to everlasting.

We have not to devise where to lay foundations, nor to design either the form of them or any part of them, much less invent some modern novel alternative to them. For when this world has passed away, when time has ceased to be, when the world to come has come to pass, when eternity is ushered in, then the walls of the holy city shall appear containing within them all that is of God; all those redeemed from among men, from out of time, from this present world; all the citizens of the heavenly Jerusalem, distinguished by having been built upon the apostolic foundation of the Christian faith.

It is for that eternal city that the apostolic foundation was laid, and for which it exists: 'And the wall of the city had twelve foundations, and in them the names of the twelve apostles of the Lamb', Revelation 21:14.

How important therefore to discern the foundations aright now, and to be built within their perimeter! Hence the apostolic church was built upon the foundation of the apostles and prophets, Jesus Christ himself being the chief corner-stone.

From this we see plainly that there is a foundation, and that there is a proper substance in which it is to be laid; that it is to carry the weight of that church which is built upon it; and that it not only supports but gives character to what rests thereupon, being the sole vindication of the correct use of the title 'church'.

Further, we see that there is no trustworthy alternative; that this true foundation was already fully laid in the apostles' times, designated and described within the holy scripture even before the last epistle was written; that this foundation encloses the only safe area, and its perimeter is the uttermost border of the walls of salvation, outside of which there is perpetual danger.

It remains to show the nature of this foundation, to indicate it clearly, and to define its parts and the sum of them beyond a peradventure and without confusion, and to do so by appealing to the apostles themselves in their writings and to no others, because it is none other than an apostolic foundation.

II

The Foundation Uncovered

IT may be—it ought to be—asked, By what method does
one arrive at the knowledge of this foundation? and again,
What proof is there that one has done so?

I answer, that because the truths of the gospel are presented
to belief as objects of faith, they cannot be subject, in their
inwardly spiritual and outwardly intangible nature, to the
unspiritual and tangible proofs required by scientific criteria.
Yet at the same time the means of determining what those
truths are should be subject to as rigid a discipline as any imposed upon scientific inquiry into natural laws and material
facts.

In what way?

Primarily by determining, separating and collating all the
evidence—strictly from the only legitimate source—relevant
to the particular gospel truth about which inquiry is to be
made; and moreover by maintaining this discipline in each
case with all the truths, the sum of which comprises the
gospel.

What evidence?

In the first instance, there is the precise meaning of the
word used in the original language describing the particular
doctrine to be understood. To determine this meaning, every

single instance in which the word concerned has been used, and no matter how often it occurs, must be carefully isolated, objectively examined, and the exact meaning precisely defined; and this also together with all the family of words of which it is a part, so that the whole scope and nuance of that word may be clearly understood without bias. Supposing the word to be found in the new testament, then furthermore it must be examined together with its Hebrew counterpart and roots; and if in the old, then with the new testament Greek equivalent. No stone must be left unturned; all this evidence must be sifted and accumulated.

Secondly, there is the meaning in each case in holy writ of the texts themselves in which the descriptive word has been found, both in the pertinent testament and in its equivalent. Not now the meaning of the word in its text, but of the drift of that text in its context. All these references must be carefully and thoroughly examined and determined in turn and place, as well as those references closely connected with those denoting the truth in question.

Moreover nothing else must be introduced. Strictly and rigidly the evidence, the whole evidence and nothing but the evidence must be gathered from the singular and sole source of holy scripture, and in the only two branches of inquiry, namely, the meaning and the use of the word concerned; and gathered without premature conclusion, previous bias, or the slightest vestige of inclination to traditional interpretation. So far as it is possible such a sifting of evidence must be wrought in the calm tranquillity of what amounts to a disciplined and isolated vacuum.

Much may be found to be irrelevant or repetitive. But as when in a pathological laboratory an obscure organism is to be isolated and identified, many carefully prepared cultures may be used to no purpose other than elimination—all results negative—yet this is regarded as positive evidence in the sense that it demonstrates what that organism is not: so with equal thoroughness must this study be disciplined. At the last we shall isolate that doctrine under inquiry, an essential truth of the gospel, and have all our relevant evidence spread before us.

Then comes the work of crystallising the essence of that evidence into a clear expression of what it conveys. This is what I mean by a systematic approach. This must be done with each single truth that is part of the truth, every single doctrine the sum of which is the doctrine.

Then finally all these truths thus opened must be laid side by side in proper proportion and in the correct order.

This is the arduous work of many years—decades—and no less is the result now to be published and presented before the judgment of the reader.

But quite apart from all this as to method, it is also vitally true that no man taketh this honour unto himself but he that is called of God. Such a person must be able to declare his regeneration, show his call to the ministry, demonstrate its fruitfulness, and manifest his divine direction to this work. Also this must be seen to be supported both by the clear force and maintenance of providence over the years, and by the sustained openings into the truth from the Spirit of God.

He will soak every page, every word, with heart-felt prayer. He will feel and be seen to feel his total inadequacy and inability in a spirit of heart-broken mortification. He will bring no earthly qualifications, no human learning or academic grading to help. He will cry from his soul, Where is boasting? It is excluded! And his language will be, No man is sufficient for these things; but God hath revealed them unto us by his Spirit.

Then and then only can men take knowledge of such, that they have been with Jesus: saying, Whence have these men letters, never having learned? and drawing the conclusion, This thing is of God!

III

What the Foundation is Not

IT is not anything modern generations can dismiss on the grounds that since the apostles laid it, and the early church was built upon it, hence automatically all subsequent ages rest thereupon—no. It is not that kind of a foundation.

Being a moral and spiritual foundation it cannot and must not be taken for granted as a past historical and structural fact, but each rising and living generation must regard it anew as a personal, moral and spiritual issue for themselves. If they value their immortal souls at all, they must discover the foundation for themselves, and must humbly, meekly but discerningly judge their contemporary church—which the foundation preceded and over which it has precedence—by what is revealed to them.

Again, because it is a moral and spiritual foundation, it is expressed not in terms of an archaic event in history but as abiding truth: hence as such it is set forth in the new testament through the writings of the apostles. These ministers of Christ preached, taught and wrote the spiritual truths constituting that foundation: believing them brought one, and still brings one, onto it. The fact that it was once delivered, does not and cannot alter its permanent application and perpetual relevance as the sole justification of a church, the church or any church, in that day, this day or any other day.

But the fact that it was men who delivered this divine revelation ought not to convey the idea of that optional variety of interpretation, flexibility of meaning and uncertainty of communication which otherwise accompanies the word of man. For it is, 'Thus saith the Lord.' It is the word of God: not of private interpretation, neither of dubious confirmation, nor yet has the shaky hand of human fallibility affected it. It is so safeguarded by divine inspiration and providence that though these liabilities are inherent in man and the letters men use to convey ideas, yet they have been prevented from affecting the word of truth, the gospel of salvation, the apostolic foundation.

But how? By many means and much every way.

One of the first means is the extraordinary men used to lay this foundation. Holy men. How rare! Men who had under-gone such humiliation, tribulation, mortification; who had not fainted under the Lord's rebuke, who had suffered the scourging of God, who had endured the chastening of the Lord. Who had learned, not how to be perfect, but how to so know themselves as to feel their inherent and subtle imperfec-tions with such self-loathing and self-distrustfulness, that recoiling from these to the perfections of Christ, being filled with the inspiration of the heavenly vision, discriminating against their own natural impulses, being borne along by the Holy Ghost, despite themselves, they wrote not the word of man but the word of God.

This foundation of the faith is therefore not subject to even the loftiest elevation of man's opinion, religious aspiration or spiritual imagination, for the basic reason that it was not these men, who laid the foundation, acting towards God but, uniquely, God acting towards, within and out of them. They were passive; it was God that was active.

Such men were the holy apostles and prophets: holy men of God. Mark that, they were holy men, sanctified, set apart. Not man's men, or party men, or church men, or the country's men: holy men. And not men of letters, parts, reputation, of ambition, pride, aspiration; no, none of these things: but the rather, of God.

These laid the foundation: holy men of God, the holy apostles—sent away from God to man—and prophets, those who spoke from God, and for him, to men; besides Jesus Christ himself the chief corner-stone: 'Behold, I lay in Zion for a foundation a stone, a tried stone, a precious corner-stone, a sure foundation', Isaiah 28:16.

How surely and certainly we can build and rest upon this sure and certain salvation in the word of it, set forth by the apostles' doctrine, precisely because it is not the word of men but the foundation of God which standeth sure, and is divinely sealed withal.

Nor yet is that foundation of the apostles one of subjective emotional experience, or the apostolic record of that experience; but rather the apostles received an objective, recorded body of truth. 'See that thou make all things according to the pattern showed to thee in the mount', could hardly be subjective; any more than a written record of the things most surely believed among us.

The fact is that this objective truth was heard, spoken, recorded and preserved for us as a written revelation. This levels against the modern and novel attitude that religion is what one feels it is. That what one believes is simply what one has experienced. In fact the present climate is one in which subjective feelings are substituted for the faith: as though faith were The Faith!

I do not deny the deep experience of the apostles, nor the spiritual inwardness of the people of God. Indeed, in the proper and relative place I shall be seen to urge a deeper experience than is commonly held to be necessary. What I do

11

assert, however, is that the apostles' experience, far from having emotional origins or being an alternative to the truth, was preceded by the Spirit of God and caused by the gospel.

But nowadays, clean contrary to this vital precedent, many hold no criteria at all. Their whole religion is what they feel. They know nothing among us—not even Jesus Christ and him crucified—only what they sense currently, and that often exaggerated. Their experience is not caused by the gospel, but is a substitute for it. It is not a question of truth causing that emotional response; for the emotions stirred up of themselves their own sensory state: and that they call religion!

What foundation is this, that changes from mood to mood, person to person, day by day, one to another? It is nothing but an ephemeral, intangible and evanescent travesty of the term.

However, the mere fact of the apostolic foundation discovers the sandy basis of such as these; as does the nature of it also of others who appear to be more objective, and have somewhat to lay in the miry clay by way of token. The latter often mock at those who know no foundation—only subjective experience—yet they themselves are standing upon nothing other than the tiny plinth of that subjectively selected, and pathetically minute, pile of traditional books which they fondly suppose to be the truth.

But, once the mote and the beam are both removed through the faith of the operation of God, what remains to be seen, and seen clearly, is that true apostolic standard which sweeps aside all such subjective presumption and presumptuous subjection by laying judgment to the line and righteousness to the plummet of that objective foundation.

Furthermore, it is a fact that much which has been wont to pass with the uninstructed for an apostolic standard is actually nothing more than the mere gleaning of subjective personal preference from the field of extinct writers and past historical movements. The resultant theological and historical patchwork, cut on the bias, is then hauled to the petard of subjective intellectual opinion on some seventeenth or maybe eighteenth-century string, to which it is firmly attached, being carefully adjusted to the stature of the string-puller, thus to be hauled up and down expediently to suit the main chance of every balmy breeze from the twentieth-century winds of change. Who, however, from the seventeenth or eighteenth century, would have thought to see today a pseudo-Calvinistic banner, hoisted by the puny withered arm of free will, to be blown about by the winds of sheer Arminian preference?

But what of the undoubtedly objective historical creeds and confessions of the Orthodox, Roman Catholic and Protestant churches, written since the death of the apostles and after the close of the scriptures?

Here at least it is not a question of substituting emotionalism for the objective expression of belief. However, the inquiry still remains—and woe be to him who blindly accepts the traditions of men simply because of venerated antiquity—do these creeds wholly answer to that foundation?

Yet, here especially, without inquiry, the uninstructed and superstitious, not to mention the blindly prejudiced, are ready to fly to tradition rather than to the infinitely older apostolic foundation, to sand rather than rock, and to man rather than God.

Take the so-called Apostles' Creed, for example.

Traditionally, the twelve are said to have written it. If so, then by premature resurrection, for it did not appear till long, long after their burial! However, lately, after so long a pretence, theological scholarship is shamed into admitting

that, 'The Apostles' Creed is, as to its form, not the produc-
tion of the apostles.'

Of course it is not!

The apostles were sent to preach and teach the gospel, not
inculcate the oft repetition of twelve haphazard sentences.
The whole gospel was what they believed; that was their
credo about which they were credible, and to which they
gave credence. What was credited by them was the word of
truth, the gospel of their salvation, in all its parts and in the
sum of the parts. But this miserably attenuated Apostles'
Creed, written long after their decease and then put into
their mouths by conniving ecclesiastics, is utterly and totally
inadequate to cover the range of the truths of the gospel; and
to say that this was the sum of the apostles' creed is incredible.

The question was, and still is, What is the gospel? For it
is that which the apostles believed. That is what contains the
whole truth concerning salvation. It is that in which the
apostolic doctrine sets forth the full knowledge of Christ. It is
only that fully delivered order and structure of the truth of the
gospel, in its sum and in each part of the sum, that can rightly
be called the apostles' creed or belief. What they believed and
taught was no haphazard set of disjointed truths left to be
arranged after their decease. The arrangement was coherent
and complete in itself within the new testament before the
departure of the apostles.

This is the apostolic foundation of the church, and nothing
else can be; and neither can anything be the church that is
not founded upon this.

The fact is that within the new testament is all that the
apostles ever wrote that is preserved for us, all that they ever
authorised, the whole of that foundation upon which the
church was ever built. Indeed that is what the new testament

writings are: the apostles' creed and belief, expressed in various letters.

The sum of them—that is, every single extant word, sentence, paragraph and letter—is preserved for us in the Holy Bible in this way, just so that we may be confident of these writings, knowing that nothing outside of them is of apostolic author-ship, nor could express what was credible to the apostles by way of faith. Whosoever believes that any apostolic writings or statements exist outside of holy writ is credulous indeed. What the apostles wrote is the new testament, which is what they believed and 'creeded', and is more than sufficient to delineate the foundation of the church.

Yet how often has expediency led men to appeal to another basis! Calvin, apparent champion of the sovereignty of God though he seemed to be, leaves much to be desired in this respect. Observing the multitude of Roman Catholics regarding with awe the Apostles' Creed, he conceived the notion that by appealing to that creed and writing upon each article of it in turn—so as to fasten a massive weight of text and ancient quotation to the venerable frame of tradition—he would demonstrate that what they blindly repeated was what *he* held, not what the clergy held who demanded this vain repetition!

The result was the 'Institutes of the Christian Religion'; the framework of which was no more than that Apostles' Creed, and the purpose, to turn his opponents' artillery upon their own ranks. That may be cleverly expedient, but in its order and framework it is not the gospel as such, being by definition an extraneous subsequent arrangement, and by nature polem-ical warfare.

So many creeds in fact are nothing more nor less than polemics. They are to counter errors that have crept into the church, or heresies that have gone out from it. As such, they are negative. They state, That is wrong; even if they go on to say why it is wrong. Not so that gospel which is the apostolic foundation of the church. The gospel is affirmative. It is yea and amen in Christ Jesus, not nay and negative in the church. I do not deny that error should be refuted and downrightly exposed, but I assert that this is not the gospel as such, but a refutation as such; and one finds many that know nothing but negative polemics.

However, the gospel is God's affirmative, is joyful tidings. As such it is not written to refute, condemn or expose—absolutely essential as these negative things are for us, once first the gospel is clearly defined to us. For primarily we must see that the gospel is declared to save sinners, bring together the saints, edify the church, and glorify God and the Father by the declaration of Jesus Christ and him crucified.

Other creeds, such as the Westminster Confession, impose a theological philosophy upon the gospel.

The learned divines of ecclesiastical eminence—attained under Caesar's patronage!—sitting in erudite concourse at the palace, could never answer the question, 'How knoweth this man letters, having never learned?' For no scripture was ever given by committee, and none shall be explained by it. God used a man on each occasion to deliver his word, and the same he does alone to explain that word.

The eminent doctors had failed to remember a lesson pressed home upon the august ecclesiastical princes on a previous occasion, namely, that the apostles were 'unlearned and ignorant men' whose sole distinction was 'that they had been with Jesus'! It was the hierarchy in concourse that sent priests and Levites from Jerusalem to the lone prophet in the wilderness with the imperious question, 'Who art thou? that we may give an answer to them that sent us.'

But concourse was held of the learned doctors and eminent divines at Westminster, and the result was a philosophical and theological framework within which to fit various truths —not the simplicity of the gospel.

Despite the undoubted virtue of parts of that Confession, and also of the broader and more cautious 'Thirty-nine Articles', we find in fact a compound of prophet and philosopher, Paul and Aristotle, Christ and Moses, of the gospel hope and the legal rule; a concocting together of gospel and law, Zion and Sinai, grace and morality, faith and works, apostolic revelation and academic learning: a confusion worse confounded to the spiritual seeker and the plain reader who look for Jerusalem above, not Athens below.

But the scriptures were not written in order that learned men, priest and scribe, doctor and ruler, should devise their own theological framework into which to fit various doctrines and liberally garnish the whole with a sprinkling of texts grasped at random irrespective of testament. The gospel is not a scattering of texts to be gathered by handfuls and thrust into the basket of man's weaving. Rather the contrary: the texts indicate, for those humble enough to go to one teacher —for one is your teacher, Christ—and learn of him, the texts, I say, indicate a garment woven without seam from top to bottom, answering to the person and work of Christ, and corresponding to his members, the sum of which is the whole body of him who saith, 'I am the truth'.

To detach texts from that context, context from that framework, that framework from his person, is to be more callous over eternal truth than were the Roman soldiers over a piece of woven cloth, to be utterly brutalised to the real nature of the new testament, in that it is not a series of disjointed texts about it, but a coherent whole, the parts of which comprise the sum.

Hence I assert, the apostolic foundation was laid for time and eternity within the apostles' lifetime, and other foundation can no man lay. The faith was once delivered to the saints

—not the scholars!—and is a composite whole comprised of the sum of the beliefs in which the saints had faith from the heart. The gospel was already delivered, known and preached within the period of the new testament writings, and no subsequent Apostles' Creed, Westminster Confession, Thirty-nine Articles, papal bull, episcopal dogma or further clerical fabrication is or can be an alternative to what is fully, wholly, exclusively and properly the foundation of the church.

IV

How the Foundation is Described

1. THE WORD OF CHRIST

THE apostolic foundation is described in various ways, none of which is more endearing to his people than 'the Word of Christ'.

This is the Word in the sense of the proper name of the Son in John 1:1, 'In the beginning was the Word, and the Word was with God, and the Word was God.' The Son himself is the Word—*logos*. His name is called, The Word of God. This Word is the logos and the ultimate logic—because he is! The Word of Christ is the reason and the final rationale—because he is! That Word is true and the absolute truth—it is he, who is the way, the life and the truth! Given this, who or what else could be the foundation? None, and nothing other than Jesus Christ and him crucified.

In that the Son is set forth by the name of the Word of Christ, the meaning is that he has been coherently expressed in speech. The Word takes in the letters of the alphabets—is composed of them—which God has chosen to be the vehicle of the revelation of Christ. In terms of the old testament foreshadowing, he is the great lesson learned under law, and fully expressed as to each letter in the 119th Psalm. He is the aleph of the creation, Genesis 1:1, and the tau of expectancy, Malachi 4:6, as shadowed under the law.

He is the Creator, without whom nothing was made that was made. The worlds were made by him; Abraham rejoiced to see his day; Isaiah saw his glory; the sacrifices depicted, the tabernacle portrayed, the temple delineated, the priesthood envisaged the truth concerning himself.

He is the summation of prophecy, the fulfilment of expectancy, the consummation of desire. He is the substance of shadow, the reality of type, the seed of Abraham, the son of David, the true Melchizedek, the Messiah. This is that—from aleph to tau—which in the first thirty-nine books of the bible manifests the Word of Christ, the one foundation for time and from it, unto eternity.

He is the alpha and the omega. He contains the law—and hides it from view! He redeems the transgressors from under it: he is not only the propitiation, but also the blood-sprinkled propitiatory. Answering the old covenant—the Word of the new testament. The word begins at alpha, and ends at omega. 'I am Alpha and Omega, the beginning and the ending, saith the Lord, which is, and which was, and which is to come, the Almighty', Revelation 1:8. The first and the last.

As such, he contains the creation, the fall, the judgment, the law, the election of Israel. As such, he overcomes Satan, vanquishes sin, defeats death, and absorbs the traumatic shock of eternal judgment in the frailty of his perfect body. As such, he is the absolute answer to every possible question, the final solution to all conceivable problems, the perfect resolution of all unsolved perplexities.

In fine, the word of the gospel is Christ expressed, the very last word that can be uttered; and hence of necessity, the Foundation of God.

Furthermore, if Christ as the Word, then Christ uttered. If uttered, then uttered of God. If finally, then God's last word:

but an uttered, expressed, manifest, recorded word. Christ made known in coherent characters, in logical symbols—the word—a readable form. I do not say in the historical parts of the new testament nor in the exhortatory sections: but set forth in the new testament distinctly and exclusively in that didactic part which manifests the doctrine of Christ, as setting forth his person and work. Not the effect of that on the saints, nor the appeals to them following on their belief of it, but the word exclusively concerning Christ himself. That setting forth his person. Therefore Christ made known in a body of truth, in objective doctrine, variously described as the word, the doctrine, the truth, the gospel, the faith, the new testament, and summed up as the apostolic foundation of the Christian church.

Consider this: there is a divinely authorised, spiritually endorsed, apostolically delivered standard and settled form of sound words obligatory on the church to maintain exactly and precisely as it was in the beginning, and recorded within the new testament writings. And yet both as to its singularity and totality, largely forgotten and complacently neglected through contented indifference, and through satisfaction with the substitution of a wide variety of optional, ecclesiastical, theological, historical, ceremonial, liturgical, and even philosophical traditions or contemporary novelties and curious inventions, in the name of evangelism, missionary enterprise, or just Jesus.

But neither sandy bottom nor false foundation, nor yet the novel absence of either basis or foundation, will ever do for them that fear God. For them there can be no room for man's opinion in salvation. It is not hit and miss, yea and nay, option and choice. It is the foundation; and there was, and is, no other foundation. If one is not built upon it, one is neither Christian nor minister, neither is that the church which rests on any basis other than this.

They who laid the foundation were given grace and apostleship, for obedience to the faith—mark that, obedience to The Faith—among all nations for his name. And they that received the apostles obeyed from the heart the form of doctrine delivered unto them, being baptised by one Spirit into one body. They were thus brought squarely to be built upon the one foundation of Jesus Christ and him crucified, as made known in the truth of the word of Christ.

Consider this word.

In the new testament writings it is called the word of the kingdom, Jesus' word, the word of this salvation, the word of the Lord, the words of the Lord Jesus, the word of his grace, the word of God. The epistles refer to the word of reconciliation, the word of truth, the word of life, the word of the truth of the gospel, the word of Christ, the apostles' word, the word of faith, wholesome words, sound words, the faithful word, the engrafted word, the prophetic word, and the sincere milk of the word.

So the word is God's, concerns Christ, is of God's kingdom, about the Lord, speaks of Jesus, of the Lord Jesus, is by the apostles. It is the word of grace, of the truth, of the truth of the gospel, is a saving word, of substitution, brings life, is truth, at once wholesome, sound, faithful, prophetic and sincere. When engrafted, it brings home all these wondrous things in blessedness to the soul. This is the faithful word of which it is recorded, 'So shall my word be that goeth forth out of my mouth'—so fruitful.

And so it comes to pass, when one is in the blessedness of being upon the verbal foundation of God, and within the walls built up from it, that

> 'Bless'd is the man whom thou dost choose,
>   and causest unto thee
> so to approach that in thy courts
>   he may a dweller be.'
>
> *Psalm 65:4 **

2. THE DOCTRINE

This word also is used to describe the nature of the apostolic foundation of the Christian church.

It refers to the body of teaching indicated by the expression, 'the doctrine of Christ', and is brought forward as proof from the new testament of the fact that there was an apostolic foundation once laid, which is to be the sole basis of reference thereafter; further, that this foundation or basis is doctrinal, and the means of communicating it is through teaching.

And what teachers were Christ and his apostles!

He taught the people not as the scribes—what with their long robes, distinctive clerical dress and revered titles—but as one having authority; and in due course commanded the apostles to teach his disciples all things whatsoever he commanded. Which they did, continuing after the ascension all things that Jesus began to do and to teach, both in the temple and in all Jerusalem, ceasing not to teach and to preach Jesus. They assembled and taught much people, teaching and preaching the word of God, and that continually. Indeed it was said of one of the apostles, 'This is the man that teacheth.' And so that apostle speaks of, 'My ways which be in Christ,

---

* From *The Psalms of the Old Testament*, Tr. John Metcalfe, The Publishing Trust. See advertising pages.

as I teach everywhere in every church.' Hence they warned every man and taught every man, so as all in every place were stablished in the faith as they had been taught.

How necessary were these teachers!

It is not too much to say that it was precisely this teaching function that was the heartbeat of the church, whose teachers were not the product of any human system of learning or earthly method of training, but were called, taught and sent as from heaven solely by Jesus Christ: his apostles. He sent them whom he had before called to be with him. It is he that 'gave some, apostles; and some, prophets; and some, evangelists; and some, pastors and teachers;' and that direct from himself in heaven to and for the church below.

We see a continuously taught church by way of an effectual teaching ministry through a known body of doctrine. But, I Timothy 2:12, no woman was suffered to teach; and only those men who were obviously sent of God, who had received their doctrine not from men, neither by man, nor through any syllabus on earth, but by the Holy Ghost from Jesus Christ. These, having been brought up and disciplined in the school of Christ, could thus command and teach, having first submitted to the teaching of the Lord Jesus and his apostles.

Hence 'These things teach' is a perpetual apostolic command to the ministers of Jesus Christ; for salvation and the church depend upon such teaching for the preservation of doctrine, discipline and the ordinances. Indeed, by the body of teaching, by the heavenly mode of preparation of the teacher, by the spiritual authority resting upon him, by the absence of all that distinguished the scribes: by these things alone may the church recognise her true sent teachers.

So much for the act of teaching. As to the substance of it, the doctrine, the body of truth which was taught: the people were astonished at Jesus' doctrine! For he saith, 'My doctrine is not mine, but his that sent me'; words of the true apostle of the new testament. Under teaching from such authority, embodied in those Spirit-sent from the ascended glory, the church continued steadfast in the apostles' doctrine: hence were not carried about with every wind of doctrine, because each and every one obeyed from the heart the form of doctrine delivered unto them.

The children of God were to continue therein, being warned that, 'Whosoever transgresseth, and abideth not in the doctrine of Christ, hath not God'; that is, he was not upon the foundation. And if any come without that doctrine, he was to be refused entrance and withheld blessing on his way. And the truth is, Christ hates bad doctrine, Revelation 2:15.

Hence those ministers who are called of Jesus Christ, subject to the apostles, are to teach—according to the pastoral epistles —sound doctrine, the words of faith and good doctrine, giving attention thereto and taking heed both to person and teaching; and no wonder, for in doing this they shall both save themselves and their hearers. Such must solemnly preach and teach in the word and in doctrine.

This is that sound, solid and serious doctrine that is the very nature of the apostolic foundation, and is according to godliness; which affects speech, behaviour and dress; which separates the meek to God himself in the church, and knows nothing of any religious organisation extraneous to it.

The called man of God, by sound doctrine learned of Jesus Christ, submissive to the apostles and instructed by them, is to use all scripture as profitable for doctrine: all! Every part: imprecatory psalms, judgment passages, the dread and solemn warnings, the deep doctrinal passages, all these too, without partiality: all scripture.

The more so because the time will come when they will not endure sound doctrine. But those well taught will be kept by the apostles' teaching; showing incorruption, speaking the truth, adorning the doctrine, refusing and refuting all error, holding fast as they have been taught the body of the truth of the apostles' doctrine, being built upon the foundation of the church precisely by such teaching, for it is in fact a doctrinal foundation.

It may be said, What is this doctrine?

To open and prove that, is the object of this work in its completeness over a series of books. But first observe well the fact that there is such a body of truth at all! For this has been so neglected by Roman Catholic, so mixed by Protestant, and so confused by separatist traditions, so forgotten by many that they know not so much as whether there be any doctrine, that the purpose in these opening pages is not to show what it is, but that it existed as such, and did so as a veritable necessity.

For this doctrine, and nothing but this doctrine, is what constituted the foundation, defined the faith, created the believer, manifested the body of Christ, distinguished the church, and was what that old-fashioned ministry taught; and taught as being received from heaven, and taught by the Holy Ghost sent down from heaven, and taught intelligibly and coherently, setting forth as a composite whole the sum of its parts.

Further observe: that the church was delineated by the reception, maintenance and defence of an objective body of doctrine upon which she was founded, and without which she was nothing, is confirmed by the word: truth. This word clearly demonstrates the apostolic foundation in its nature, and hence I proceed to show this from its use.

3. THE TRUTH

The promise of Messiah to his disciples is, 'Ye shall know the truth, and the truth shall make you free.' Mark that, the truth is what does it, and freedom is what it does. As to what the truth is: it is the doctrine of Christ, who said, 'I am the truth.' The people of God are sanctified by the truth. Said Jesus, 'Thy word is truth.' By manifestation of the truth the apostles preached, not the truth of their experience, but the truth of Christ which when believed caused that experience: it was called the word of truth.

The saints obeyed the truth, and the Spirit came upon them after they heard the word of truth. Indeed, they shall all be damned who receive not the love of the truth. But, blessed be God, the saints are chosen to salvation through sanctification of the Spirit and belief of the truth. And of course, therefore, salvation is to come to the knowledge—note that, knowledge —of the truth.

No wonder the apostolic church was the pillar and ground of the truth. Her ministers were workmen rightly dividing the word of truth. Her saints were begotten by the word of truth. Hence, if we are to be of that one united, divinely authorised, apostolically founded but humanly despised church, we must obey the truth through the Spirit, and thereafter walk in the truth. This is that defined body of doctrine setting forth the Son of God. It is the truth concerning himself. It is called: the gospel.

4. THE GOSPEL

The truth is referred to as 'the gospel' some ninety times, and it is true that the gospel is another way in which to describe the apostolic foundation of the Christian church.

The gospel is that foundation, and is defined as the message of gladness; and if a message, then content is implied, coherently written and not subject to alteration by the messengers, to be delivered to the recipients just as conveyed, and wholly as conveyed, by the author. There is no guesswork, subjecting it to experience, rending it piecemeal, giving one's opinion of it. There was a message given, it was to be conveyed, and precisely that—the truth, the whole truth, and nothing but the truth—exactly to be delivered. The ministers of the gospel are not authors, but messengers of the Author of the faith.

This gospel is described as the gospel of the kingdom, the gospel of Jesus Christ, the gospel of the grace of God, the gospel of God, the gospel of Christ, the gospel of your salvation, the gospel of peace, the gospel of our Lord Jesus Christ, the glorious gospel of the blessed God.

This variety of description plainly shows the profound and manifold character of the gospel. And no wonder, for it is wholly of God and from him; it concerns the person of the Lord Jesus Christ, and is exclusive to his person; and it has in view his inheritance. It is the message of gladness, containing the setting forth of Jesus Christ by the word of truth, the gospel of our salvation: upon this the true church is founded, and by it the great professing church in all its branches is to be judged, for it has clean departed therefrom.

The contents of the gospel are called: the word of the gospel, the glorious gospel, not another gospel, the truth of the gospel, the mystery of the gospel, the faith of the gospel, the word of the truth of the gospel, the hope of the gospel, and an everlasting gospel. Once more the variety of description reveals the rich content of the thing described.

It had been preached before to Abraham, it was then being preached to Jew and Gentile, and should be preached to every creature and to regions beyond; preached without deviation, addition or subtraction; preached by gospel preachers as stones cut without hands, distinguished in that their call, preparation, sending and ministry were like their message: out of heaven from God, by Jesus Christ on high, and through the Holy Ghost alone below.

This gospel was in the form of sound words, not notions about either form or words, nor optional speculation in place of them—the things most surely believed among us; notice that: the things believed. And if believed, then that which is believed is designated: The Faith. Already we have seen the apostolic foundation to be a verity of absolute necessity: it is The Faith. The briefest examination of this will confirm how vital it is to be built upon the foundation of the apostles and prophets to the exclusion of all else.

5. The Faith

This is that which is not only believed among us, but surely so; and moreover, most surely believed! It is what is believed or creeded, the whole of it and nothing but it. It is the true apostolic creed, as opposed to the later conjectures of theological, ethical, philosophical, legal, moralistic or sacramental systems of men, with the larding into them of smatterings of bare statements and texts snapped up at random out of the great body of the whole truth as it is in Jesus.

It was fully delivered, believed on in the world, credited by the church, long before the apostles died and the scriptures closed, pre-dating in time by as much as it is richer in content the flimsy inventions of hundreds of years later, gleaned from the edges long after the harvest had gone.

The saints are to be sound in the faith, that faith of ancient, biblical and apostolic tradition; not in the inventions of ignorant ecclesiastics in the scholastic novelties that followed one after the other centuries later, dropped from various academic eminences, and were dishonestly dubbed with all kinds of titles, names and elevated distinctions, as though equal to the faith once delivered; as though implying it were not delivered.

At the very beginning in fact, in Acts, many of the Jewish priests were found obedient to the faith; the apostles exhorted the saints to continue in the faith. If so, it must have been delivered for this to have been possible. Then it follows, if delivered, already set forth within the gospels and the epistles, the sole and only record of the apostles' true creed, the sole and only apostolic writings extant, the sole and only sum of the apostolic faith.

The churches were established in that faith, and heard the apostles concerning the faith in Christ. The ministers of Christ were sent for the obedience of the faith, that which was already being fully declared, the objective word of faith. Who did not hear this, could not believe it. How shall they hear without a preacher? Whoso is called a believer, without a definition of what is believed, is an impostor. A believer by definition believes something. If it be asked, What? I say, The Faith!

If one objects, 'Away with all this doctrine! I simply believe Christ.' I answer, So did the early saints, but with this difference: they knew from whom and how they had received the truth, they knew him whom they believed, and they knew what was declared about his person and work; and they called *it*, not him, The Faith: it was about him. Whoso substitutes his bare name for it, has a Christ of his own inventing, and says, Lo, here is Christ! Go not after them. But the true Christ is declared by things most surely believed. The gospel, it, is the power of God unto salvation. God's Son is known by the truth, not without it. And the truth is declared in the faith, not the option.

Hence even then, the unruly and disobedient to the apostolic authority were to examine themselves whether they be in the faith. The apostles were continually to preach the faith; the saints to strive—mark that, strive—together for the faith, to continue in it and be established therein.

It is the defined faith, not the imagined sentiment, which is in Christ Jesus; although some would depart from the faith, deny the faith, err from the faith; others overthrow the faith of some; and the worst would be reprobate concerning the faith. So observe, all have not the faith of our Lord Jesus Christ who make a Christian profession; in fact multitudes but take the name and deny or contradict the faith. Such we are to resist steadfast in the faith, unmoved; for it was once delivered to the saints long before scripture closed.

The apostolic foundation was already declared for faith within the new testament; and is there, and only there, fully set forth that we may be kept sound in the faith which is in Christ Jesus. This is that form of sound words—mark it, form— called variously the faith, the word of faith, the unity of the faith, the mystery of the faith, the words of faith and good doctrine, the faith of our Lord Jesus Christ, and the faith once delivered to the saints.

6. THE NEW TESTAMENT

A testament is by definition a document to be opened after death, distributing blessing to the beneficiaries. So is the new covenant; that between the Father and the Son, of which Christ is mediator, the one mediator, the mediator of the new testament.

He is the apostle of our profession who declares the terms of the covenant, as well as the testator whose will is ratified in blood, but thereafter declared by able ministers of the new testament called and equipped to declare the blessings brought in for the heirs of faith. This is the foundation. And as we have seen, it is an objective basis altogether.

7. The Foundation

The church, that is alone worthy the name, and heir to the benefits, is built upon the apostolic foundation. However, this building is spiritual, and also so is the foundation upon which it rests.

Naturally, however, a foundation is by definition a precisely defined and measured area, excavated of all that is earthy and brought down to bedrock—for the soundness of the site is as important as that of the foundations themselves—so that it is able to take the great weight later to rise upon it. The building of foundations commences out of sight beneath the surface of the earth, up from the rock which has been bared, to level with the surface of the ground. Only such sound, stable and deep foundations are able to take the weight of the successive stories to rise thereupon; and also only such can give security from stress of storm, tempest, flood and earthquake when they come, as come they must.

This is in the spiritual sense precisely the function of the apostolic foundation. Nothing but this foundation—upon that site called 'holy mountains'—can take the weight of the church of God both for time and eternity; and nothing else bear the stress when the rain of fiery judgment descends, and the floods of vindictive wrath come, and the winds of furious vengeance blow, and beat thereon.

Then, then what is built upon the rock shall stand and those within the walls shall be safe, when all else shall collapse and everyone else shall be lost.

Then, then the proof of what is set before the reader will be amply vindicated and justified in the event.

The apostles have bared the rock from all that is of the earth, and within a carefully defined area have dug down and built up the solid foundation of apostolic doctrine. In their writings there is nothing of the flesh or of the world or that is earthly; all has been excavated. There remains solely what is of God. But not haphazardly so; for they have in the word of the truth of the gospel given us clear lines on which to build, clear definitions on which to rest. Not upon what is merely traditional, ecclesiastical, historical, national or geographical—all that must be excavated too. For we must come to rest upon the spiritual basis of sole recognition of that integral apostles' doctrine, and belief from the heart in the same.

That is the basis of the church, and the only one, the foundation which is fully complete within itself. This the apostle once laid, and recorded the laying of it: 'I have laid the foundation', I Corinthians 3:10. No man ever can lay another. If he says he does, or points to another, he is a false apostle, a deceitful worker. We are to be built upon the apostolic foundation, if we are to be in and of the church at all, Ephesians 2:20.

Furthermore, it is obligatory upon us to answer as one building to that spiritual reality. The kind of slum of squatters' shacks in higgledy-piggledy chaos independently littering the field today is evidence of not being built on one foundation, if it is evidence of anything at all.

But the one foundation once laid is the foundation of God, II Timothy 2:19. It standeth sure. Abraham looked for it when he sought a city which hath foundations, whose builder and maker is God. And if Abraham's seed today look for the same, and not at the things and churches which can be seen, they too shall discern by faith as pilgrims what cannot be seen by sight as residents.

The walls of the heavenly city have foundations: twelve, to be precise; and they are doubtless laid by the apostles, for in them are their names. Since at the beginning of the church these foundations of doctrine were laid, and since at the end of the age in eternity nothing remains in glory but what is above and upon these foundations, I say to my soul, and to him that feareth God, Take heed how ye are built thereon!

V

Being Built upon the Foundation

BY the foregoing manifold proofs I have shown beyond all reasonable doubt that there is one foundation for the Christian church, and that this foundation is objective: it is outside of ourselves, and of course outside of the church or churches which, by its very presence, it either justifies or condemns in any given age.

This foundation is not subject to any consequent dictates of the church, which has neither right nor authority to ignore, add, subtract, multiply, divide, or otherwise alter it. For in so doing, ecclesiastics tamper with the eternal salvation of the immortal souls, putting them at dire peril, of those that blindly trust in the church of itself automatically to be faithful and true. The truth is, the professing church has proved faithless and false, and only Christ remains as Faithful and True, Revelation 19:11.

In the nature of building, of necessity the foundation is prior to that which is built upon it, and provides the sole justification, judgment and *raison d'être* at any time of any given church and of all the service and services of that church.

Moreover the apostolic foundation is of itself not experimental but doctrinal, and the only authorised religious organisation or structure following after it is that church which is built upon it: for this structure not being open to opinion, neither subject to what is geographical, historical or traditional, is in fact apostolically doctrinal, and exclusively limited in the future to that which was from the beginning.

The foundation stands in truth, inviting belief. It is itself total and complete within itself. The first sentence has been written and the last word uttered. This doctrinal, external, objective and spiritual foundation has been laid, can be defined, is capable of precise location, and is subject to definite proof. It is to be referred to constantly with the objective critical faculty by those that would follow in the way of right-eousness, and be built within the walls of salvation.

But that said, it is still true that Christ is the builder, not men. 'Upon this rock I will build my church', saith Christ. I will; mark that. 'Except the Lord'—not only design the foundation, but—'build the house, they labour in vain that build it.' Certainly the chief and great mark that the Lord is building is the spiritual awareness of, and constant reference to, the foundation of the faith, on the part of those being built into a spiritual house; but the point now being made is that Christ himself at present in spirit is the builder.

Whenever and wherever Christ builds, he builds upon the foundation of the apostles and prophets, 'Jesus Christ himself being the chief corner-stone, in whom all the building fitly framed together groweth unto an holy temple in the Lord, in whom ye also'—who are so built today—'are builded together for an habitation of God through the Spirit.' This does not refer to some traditional historical church or denomination. It refers to that which at any given point in time is built on that foundation and upon nothing else, for either doctrine, fellowship or the ordinances, as applying to Christian, church or the ministry.

The point is that Christ builds, and does so through the defined doctrine of that one foundation, clearly laid out objectively. Still, if Christ in person himself does the building, then from on high he does so by the Spirit below, clearly marked subectively. As saith the ancient prophet, 'So shall my word be that goeth forth out of my mouth', Isaiah 55:11. My word—that is one thing; and a thing once given, then uttered, and finally recorded. That goeth forth out of my mouth—that is another thing; and is a recurring conveyance of that word to the earth, so as by it actually to effect immense fruitfulness.

For it is not a question of God's word out of man's mouth, nor even God's word out of the church's mouth. Man as such is not only not the founder, but equally neither is he the builder. Christ is the builder: 'I will build my church', not the church will build itself. 'My word out of my mouth', not my word out of men's mouths that elect themselves speakers. It is therefore God's word out of God's mouth that spiritually raises the house of God. It is all of God, from first to last.

By preaching is God's house raised up, and Christ is seen as the speaker. See that ye refuse not him that speaketh from heaven. I do not deny that he uses his apostles and ministers; but assert that it is he that calls, prepares, sends and uses them, not they that use themselves. He speaks inwardly whilst using them outwardly; and he does so in such a way as to strip all glory and possibility of boasting from them and from the church, and to bring all the glory to himself. 'Today if ye will hear his voice, harden not your hearts.'

Under this preaching, Christ's subjective voice directs us onto that objective foundation once laid. Through the preaching, Christ so puts the truth of that word in the mouth of those sent and used by himself, that the foundation of the faith is clearly perceived by the hearers.

So that if there is declared in the foundation the knowledge of Christ, still, it is the Son of God himself who uses that knowledge to convey 'a spirit of wisdom and revelation in the knowledge of him'. Flesh and blood, as Peter learned, had not revealed it; no, the Father reveals the Son by an inward revelation that is spiritually communicated through the word: on this rock the church is built. 'Upon this rock I will build my church.'

The rock *in* which it is built is the rock of the immutable counsel, the incontrovertible oath, the irresistible will, the everlasting covenant, the eternal purpose, the absolute decree and the inscrutable election of God. 'His foundation is in the holy mountains', Psalm 87:1.

The rock *on* which the church is built, is that rock of the foundation itself, which is sunk and keyed into the previously-mentioned rock of the holy mountains. And since 'other foundation can no man lay than that is laid, which is Jesus Christ', it follows, 'that Rock was Christ', I Cor. 10:4.

Christ Jesus is the rock of offence to the self-righteous, the shadow of a great rock to poor sinners, the LORD my rock to King David, and the rock of their salvation to the elect. The foundation-rock of the church is Jesus Christ and him crucified. It is this that Peter confesses in faith: 'Thou art the Christ, the Son of the living God.' As saith the 62nd Psalm, 'He only is my rock and my salvation.'

The building *upon* that rock is the immediate inward revelation of the Holy Ghost lighting up that foundation to the inner man with the inward light of God's glory. It is the revelation of the mystery. It is God shining into our hearts to give the knowledge of the glory of God in the face of Jesus Christ. 'Blessed art thou, Simon Bar-jona: for flesh and blood hath not revealed it unto thee, but my Father which is in heaven.' This is the hiding of these things from the wise and prudent, and revealing them unto babes. It is the opening of the eyes of the blind. It is that which the Holy Ghost teacheth. And it is with this revelation upon that foundation that Christ builds his church.

Hence the apostle declares that it pleased God—God, notice —to call him by his grace, and reveal—by revelation, observe —his Son in Paul. And Paul, who informed the Corinthian church of the one foundation laid in apostolic doctrine, also insists as to their being built thereon: God hath revealed these things unto us by his Spirit.

This secret inward and spiritual voice of Christ accompanies the true preaching of the evangel by those whom he has sent even unto this day; and as stated, it answers to Isaiah's 'out of my mouth'. The mouth of Christ is that out of which goeth a sharp two-edged sword; yet there is such a range of utterance that, 'The roof of thy mouth is like the best wine'. Hence those who have tasted that the Lord is gracious are moved to say, 'Let him kiss me with the kisses of his mouth'. Grace is poured into his lips, as we feel when he breathes immediately and feelingly upon our souls; and in this experience we declare, 'His mouth is most sweet'. So captivated with this soul-ravishing experience of his living presence are those who feel it, that they wax rapturous in the sense of it: 'His cheeks are as a bed of spices, as sweet flowers; his lips like lilies, dropping sweet-smelling myrrh.'

From the mouth of the Son of God in heaven, goes forth by the Spirit of God on earth, that externally inaudible but internally discernible voice that calls us in the heart-enlarging ecstasy of the knowledge of salvation. This wonderful revelation of and from his real and living person is a secret internal answer to the public external preaching of that precise, defined and objective declaration of the knowledge of himself, his person and work, in the foundation of the faith.

So it comes to pass that, 'The dead shall hear the voice of the Son of God: and they that hear shall live.' It is in fact those who hear his voice that are built upon this foundation; and in this way, his sheep hear his voice and follow him. They are directed by that voice in the once-delivered faith, onto the once-laid foundation, through the word of the truth of the gospel, as declared by the preaching of those sent and used by himself.

And these sheep make no mistake. They know his voice, sounding inwardly, co-operative with the external preaching of the gospel by ministers sent of Christ to this day. Others may hear nothing but the audible words of a visible preacher, finding their religion in intellectual appreciation at most. But not so those sheep that know him, and are known of him: these hear not only his word, but his voice therein.

Hence it is said, 'Today if ye will hear his voice, harden not your hearts.' Mark that, today, not yesterday; and hear, not read; finally, voice, not writing. Therefore, quite distinct from the fact of preaching from a material bible by the physical voice of the tangible preacher in a visible meeting: now, today, immediately, the present voice of Christ glorified in heaven mysteriously sounds also on earth inwardly speaking by the Spirit.

It is in this way that we discern the Holy Ghost anointing, filling and giving unction to those preachers whom Christ has himself called, gifted and prepared; the Spirit using their preaching to glorify Christ by imparting an inward and vital reality to the things externally described, a lively experience within of the person audibly set forth without, a heavenly vision to the scriptural description of the things most surely believed among us. This is his manner of teaching, and brings all the glory to God, and excludes all boasting completely from man, for none teacheth like him.

As to that secret spiritual sound of Christ's voice in the hidden parts of the inward man of the heart, it is said, 'He that hath ears to hear, let him hear.'

Hear what? The gospel? Yes, that; but then the external ears will serve that purpose: so consequently this must refer to the inward hearing. Hear what then? What the churches say? What the clergy say? What the historical Reformation said?

The book of Revelation instructs us, 'Hear what the Spirit saith unto the churches.' And if the faithful in the churches were directed—despite those churches and what they said—to hear the Spirit then, with the apostle still alive, how much more now?

As it was then, so today. Only by this faithful, renewing, Christ-glorifying Holy Spirit, eternal and unchanged in his person and his work, are they that love the truth reliably led in the gospel onto the one foundation, having a witness to the same. By the Spirit alone are they quickened, regenerate, converted, sanctified, preserved, and led into all truth. They who listen, hear his voice, hear Christ's voice, and are comforted in the hearing of the word of faith; for did they not at the beginning receive the Spirit through the hearing of faith? And moreover, the Holy Ghost fell on all them who heard the word. So shall God's word be that goeth forth out of his mouth: a fruitful word.

Hence today, if ye will hear his present immediate voice, know that it will accompany nothing but the true, faithful, God-fearing preaching of the apostolic doctrine, and that, only by those sent of God. That voice will direct you by this preaching into the knowledge of Christ with those gathering together in him.

It is this that will establish you upon the once-laid foundation, able to bear the weight of your soul for time and eternity; which may God of his mercy grant the reader. And to such we say, 'He which stablisheth us with you in Christ, and hath anointed us, is God; who hath also sealed us, and given the earnest of the Spirit in our hearts.' Amen.

JOHN METCALFE

INDEX

TO OTHER PUBLICATIONS

ii

PSALMS, HYMNS AND SPIRITUAL SONGS

THE PSALMS

OF THE

OLD TESTAMENT

The Psalms of the Old Testament, the result of years of painstaking labour, is an original translation into verse from the Authorised Version, which seeks to present the Psalms in the purest scriptural form possible for singing. Here, for the first time, divine names are rendered as and when they occur in the scripture, the distinction between LORD and Lord has been preserved, and every essential point of doctrine and experience appears with unique perception and fidelity.

The Psalms of the Old Testament is the first part of a trilogy written by John Metcalfe, the second part of which is entitled *Spiritual Songs from the Gospels*, and the last, *The Hymns of the New Testament*. These titles provide unique and accurate metrical versions of passages from the psalms, the gospels and the new testament epistles respectively, and are intended to be used together in the worship of God.

Price £2.50 *(postage extra)*
(hard-case binding, dust-jacket)
Printed, sewn and bound
by the John Metcalfe Publishing Trust
ISBN 0 9506366 7 3

SPIRITUAL SONGS
FROM
THE GOSPELS

The *Spiritual Songs from the Gospels*, the result of years of painstaking labour, is an original translation into verse from the Authorised Version, which seeks to present essential parts of the gospels in the purest scriptural form possible for singing. The careful selection from Matthew, Mark, Luke and John, set forth in metrical verse of the highest integrity, enables the singer to sing 'the word of Christ' as if from the scripture itself, 'richly and in all wisdom'; and, above all, in a way that facilitates worship in song of unprecedented fidelity.

The *Spiritual Songs from the Gospels* is the central part of a trilogy written by John Metcalfe, the first part of which is entitled *The Psalms of the Old Testament*, and the last, *The Hymns of the New Testament*. These titles provide unique and accurate metrical versions of passages from the psalms, the gospels and the new testament epistles respectively, and are intended to be used together in the worship of God.

Price £2.50 *(postage extra)*
(hard-case binding, dust-jacket)
Printed, sewn and bound
by the John Metcalfe Publishing Trust
ISBN 0 9506366 8 1

THE HYMNS

OF THE

NEW TESTAMENT

The *Hymns of the New Testament*, the result of years of painstaking labour, is an original translation into verse from the Authorised Version, which presents essential parts of the new testament epistles in the purest scriptural form possible for singing. The careful selection from the book of Acts to that of Revelation, set forth in metrical verse of the highest integrity, enables the singer to sing 'the word of Christ' as if from the scripture itself, 'richly and in all wisdom'; and, above all, in a way that facilitates worship in song of unprecedented fidelity.

The *Hymns of the New Testament* is the last part of a trilogy written by John Metcalfe, the first part of which is entitled *The Psalms of the Old Testament*, and the next, *Spiritual Songs from the Gospels*. These titles provide unique and accurate metrical versions of passages from the psalms, the gospels and the new testament epistles respectively, and are intended to be used together in the worship of God.

Price £2.50 *(postage extra)*
(hard-case binding, dust-jacket)
Printed, sewn and bound
by the John Metcalfe Publishing Trust
ISBN 0 9506366 9 X

'THE APOSTOLIC FOUNDATION OF THE CHRISTIAN CHURCH' SERIES

x

Since selling out the entire stock
of all previous printings,
the Trust is glad to announce
this new 1993 enlarged impression

FOUNDATIONS UNCOVERED

THE APOSTOLIC FOUNDATION
OF THE
CHRISTIAN CHURCH

Volume I

Foundations Uncovered is the introduction to the major series: 'The Apostolic Foundation of the Christian Church'.

Rich in truth, the Introduction deals comprehensively with the foundation of the apostolic faith under the descriptive titles: The Word, The Doctrine, The Truth, The Gospel, The Faith, The New Testament, and The Foundation.

The contents of the book reveal: The Fact of the Foundation; The Foundation Uncovered; What the Foundation is not; How the Foundation is Described; and, Being Built upon the Foundation.

'This book comes with the freshness of a new Reformation.'

Price 75p *(postage extra)*
(Laminated cover)
Printed, sewn and bound
by the John Metcalfe Publishing Trust
ISBN 0 9506366 5 7

*To meet constant and world-wide demand
for this 'Truly great Christian work'
since selling out the entire stock
of all previous printings, the Trust
is glad to announce a completely new
1993 second edition, thoroughly revised*

THE BIRTH OF JESUS CHRIST

THE APOSTOLIC FOUNDATION
OF THE
CHRISTIAN CHURCH

Volume II

'The very spirit of adoration and worship rings through the pages of *The Birth of Jesus Christ.*

'The author expresses with great clarity the truths revealed to him in his study of holy scriptures at depth. We are presented here with a totally lofty view of the Incarnation.

'John Metcalfe is to be classed amongst the foremost expositors of our age; and his writings have about them that quality of timelessness that makes me sure they will one day take their place among the heritage of truly great Christian works.'

From a review by Rev. David Catterson.

'Uncompromisingly faithful to scripture ... has much to offer which is worth serious consideration ... deeply moving.'

The Expository Times.

Price 95p *(postage extra)*
(Laminated Cover)
Printed, sewn and bound
by the John Metcalfe Publishing Trust
ISBN 1 870039 48 3

THE MESSIAH

THE APOSTOLIC FOUNDATION
OF THE
CHRISTIAN CHURCH

Volume III

The Messiah is a spiritually penetrating and entirely original exposition of Matthew chapter one to chapter seven from the trenchant pen of John Metcalfe.

Matthew Chapters One to Seven

GENEALOGY · BIRTH · STAR OF BETHLEHEM
HEROD · FLIGHT TO EGYPT · NAZARETH
JOHN THE BAPTIST · THE BAPTIST'S MINISTRY
JESUS' BAPTISM · ALL RIGHTEOUSNESS FULFILLED
HEAVEN OPENED · THE SPIRIT'S DESCENT
THE TEMPTATION OF JESUS IN THE WILDERNESS
JESUS' MANIFESTATION · THE CALLING · THE TRUE DISCIPLES
THE BEATITUDES · THE SERMON ON THE MOUNT

'Something of the fire of the ancient Hebrew prophet .... Metcalfe has spiritual and expository potentials of a high order.'

The Life of Faith.

Price £2.45 *(postage extra)*
(425 pages, Laminated Cover)
ISBN 0 9502515 8 5

THE SON OF GOD AND SEED OF DAVID

THE APOSTOLIC FOUNDATION
OF THE
CHRISTIAN CHURCH

Volume IV

The Son of God and Seed of David is the fourth volume in the major work entitled 'The Apostolic Foundation of the Christian Church.'

'The author proceeds to open and allege that Jesus Christ is and ever was *The Son of God*. This greatest of subjects, this most profound of all mysteries, is handled with reverence and with outstanding perception.

'The second part considers *The Seed of David*. What is meant precisely by 'the seed'? And why 'of David'? With prophetic insight the author expounds these essential verities.'

Price £6.95 *(postage extra)*
Hardback 250 pages
Laminated bookjacket
Printed, sewn and bound
by the John Metcalfe Publishing Trust
ISBN 1 870039 16 5

CHRIST CRUCIFIED

THE APOSTOLIC FOUNDATION
OF THE
CHRISTIAN CHURCH

Volume V

Christ Crucified the definitive work on the crucifixion, the blood, and the cross of Jesus Christ.

The crucifixion of Jesus Christ witnessed in the Gospels: the gospel according to Matthew; Mark; Luke; John.

The blood of Jesus Christ declared in the Epistles: the shed blood; the blood of purchase; redemption through his blood; the blood of sprinkling; the blood of the covenant.

The doctrine of the cross revealed in the apostolic foundation of the Christian church: the doctrine of the cross; the cross and the body of sin; the cross and the carnal mind; the cross and the law; the offence of the cross; the cross of our Lord Jesus Christ.

Price £6.95 *(postage extra)*
Hardback 300 pages
Laminated bookjacket
Printed, sewn and bound
by the John Metcalfe Publishing Trust
ISBN 1 870039 08 4

JUSTIFICATION BY FAITH

THE APOSTOLIC FOUNDATION
OF THE
CHRISTIAN CHURCH

Volume VI

THE HEART OF THE GOSPEL · THE FOUNDATION OF THE CHURCH
THE ISSUE OF ETERNITY
CLEARLY, ORIGINALLY AND POWERFULLY OPENED

The basis · The righteousness of the law
The righteousness of God · The atonement · Justification
Traditional views considered · Righteousness imputed to faith
Faith counted for righteousness · Justification by Faith

'And it came to pass, when Jesus had ended these sayings, the people were astonished at his doctrine: for he taught them as one having authority, and not as the scribes.' Matthew 7:28,29.

Price £7.50 *(postage extra)*
Hardback 375 pages
Laminated bookjacket
Printed, sewn and bound
by the John Metcalfe Publishing Trust
ISBN 1870039 11 4

THE CHURCH: WHAT IS IT?

THE APOSTOLIC FOUNDATION
OF THE
CHRISTIAN CHURCH

Volume VII

The answer to this question proceeds first from the lips of Jesus himself, Mt. 16:18, later to be expounded by the words of the apostles whom he sent.

Neither fear of man nor favour from the world remotely affect the answer.

Here is the truth, the whole truth, and nothing but the truth.

The complete originality, the vast range, and the total fearlessness of this book command the attention in a way that is unique.

Read this book: you will never read another like it.

Outspokenly devastating yet devastatingly constructive.

Price £7.75 *(postage extra)*
Hardback 400 pages
Laminated bookjacket
Printed, sewn and bound
by the John Metcalfe Publishing Trust
ISBN 1 870039 23 8

xviii

OTHER TITLES

NOAH AND THE FLOOD

Noah and the Flood expounds with vital urgency the man and the message that heralded the end of the old world. The description of the flood itself is vividly realistic. The whole work has an unmistakable ring of authority, and speaks as 'Thus saith the Lord'.

'Mr. Metcalfe makes a skilful use of persuasive eloquence as he challenges the reality of one's profession of faith ... he gives a rousing call to a searching self-examination and evaluation of one's spiritual experience.'
The Monthly Record of the Free Church of Scotland.

Price £1.90 *(postage extra)*
(Laminated Cover)
Printed, sewn and bound
by the John Metcalfe Publishing Trust
ISBN 1 870039 22 X

DIVINE FOOTSTEPS

Divine Footsteps traces the pathway of the feet of the Son of man from the very beginning in the prophetic figures of the true in the old testament through the reality in the new; doing so in a way of experimental spirituality. At the last a glimpse of the coming glory is beheld as his feet are viewed as standing at the latter day upon the earth.

Price 95p *(postage extra)*
(Laminated Cover)
Printed, sewn and bound
by the John Metcalfe Publishing Trust
ISBN 1 870039 21 1

THE RED HEIFER

The Red Heifer was the name given to a sacrifice used by the children of Israel in the Old Testament—as recorded in Numbers 19—in which a heifer was slain and burned. Cedar wood, hyssop and scarlet were cast into the burning, and the ashes were mingled with running water and put in a vessel. It was kept for the children of Israel for a water of separation: it was a purification for sin.

In this unusual book the sacrifice is brought up to date and its relevance to the church today is shown.

Price 75p *(postage extra)*
ISBN 0 9502515 4 2

THE WELLS OF SALVATION

The Wells of Salvation is written from a series of seven powerful addresses preached at Tylers Green. It is a forthright and experimental exposition of Isaiah 12:3, 'Therefore with joy shall ye draw water out of the wells of salvation.'

John Metcalfe is acknowledged to be perhaps the most gifted expositor and powerful preacher of our day and this is to be seen clearly in The Wells of Salvation.

Price £1.50 *(postage extra)*
(Laminated Cover)
ISBN 0 9502515 6 9

OF GOD OR MAN?

LIGHT FROM GALATIANS

The Epistle to the Galatians contends for deliverance from the law and from carnal ministry.

The Apostle opens his matter in two ways:

Firstly, Paul vindicates himself and his ministry against those that came not from God above, but from Jerusalem below.

Secondly, he defends the Gospel and evangelical liberty against legal perversions and bondage to the flesh.

Price £1.45 *(postage extra)*
(Laminated Cover)
ISBN 0 9506366 3 0

A QUESTION FOR POPE JOHN PAUL II

As a consequence of his many years spent apart in prayer, lonely vigil, and painstaking study of the scripture, John Metcalfe asks a question and looks for an answer from Pope John Paul II.

Price £1.25. *(postage extra)*
(Laminated Cover)
ISBN 0 9506366 4 9

THE BOOK OF RUTH

The Book of Ruth is set against the farming background of old testament Israel at the time of the Judges, the narrative—unfolding the work of God in redemption—being marked by a series of agricultural events.

These events—the famine; the barley harvest; the wheat harvest; the winnowing—possessed a hidden spiritual significance to that community, but, much more, they speak in figure directly to our own times, as the book reveals.

Equally contemporary appear the characters of Ruth, Naomi, Boaz, and the first kinsman, drawn with spiritual perception greatly to the profit of the reader.

Price £4.95 *(postage extra)*
Hardback 200 pages
Laminated bookjacket
Printed, sewn and bound
by the John Metcalfe Publishing Trust
ISBN 1 870039 17 3

PRESENT-DAY CONVERSIONS
OF THE NEW TESTAMENT KIND

FROM THE MINISTRY OF

JOHN METCALFE

The outstandingly striking presentation of this fascinating paperback will surely catch the eye, as its title and contents will certainly captivate the mind: here is a unique publication.

Woven into a gripping narrative, over twenty-one short life stories, all centred on conversions that simply could not have happened had not God broken in, and had not Christ been revealed, the book presents a tremendous challenge, at once moving and thrilling to the reader.

Price £2.25 (postage extra)
(Laminated Cover)
Printed, sewn and bound
by the John Metcalfe Publishing Trust
ISBN 1 870039 31 9

DIVINE MEDITATIONS

OF

WILLIAM HUNTINGTON

Originally published by Mr. Huntington as a series of letters to J. Jenkins, under the title of 'Contemplations on the God of Israel', the spiritual content of this correspondence has been skilfully and sympathetically edited, abridged, and arranged so as to form a series of meditations, suitable for daily readings.

Mr. Huntington's own text is thereby adapted to speak directly to the reader in a way much more suited to his ministering immediately to ourselves, in our own circumstances and times.

It is greatly hoped that many today will benefit from this adaption which carefully retains both the spirit and the letter of the text. If any prefer the original format, this is readily available from several sources and many libraries.

Nevertheless, the publishers believe the much more readable form into which Mr. Huntington's very words have been adapted will appeal to a far wider audience, for whose comfort and consolation this carefully edited work has been published.

Price £2.35 *(postage extra)*
(Laminated Cover)
Printed, sewn and bound
by the John Metcalfe Publishing Trust
ISBN 1 870039 24 6

SAVING FAITH

The sevenfold work of the Holy Ghost in bringing a sinner to saving faith in Christ opened and enlarged.

True faith is the work of God. False faith is the presumption of man. But where is the difference? *Saving Faith* shows the difference.

Price £2.25 *(postage extra)*
Paperback 250 pages
(Laminated Cover)
Printed, sewn and bound
by the John Metcalfe Publishing Trust
ISBN 1 870039 40 8

DELIVERANCE FROM THE LAW
THE WESTMINSTER CONFESSION EXPLODED

Deliverance from the law. A devastating vindication of the gospel of Christ against the traditions of man.

Price £1.90 *(postage extra)*
Paperback 160 pages
(Laminated Cover)
Printed, sewn and bound
by the John Metcalfe Publishing Trust
ISBN 1 870039 41 6

NEWLY PUBLISHED

THE BEATITUDES

A unique insight destined to be the classic opening of this wonderful sequence of utterances from the lips of Jesus.

The reader will discover a penetration of the spiritual heights and divine depths of these peerless words in a way ever fresh and always rewarding though read time and time again.

Price £1.90 *(postage extra)*
Paperback 185 pages
(Laminated cover)
Printed, sewn and bound
by the John Metcalfe Publishing Trust
ISBN 1 870039 45 9

'TRACT FOR THE TIMES' SERIES

THE GOSPEL OF GOD

'TRACT FOR THE TIMES' SERIES

The Gospel of God. Beautifully designed, this tract positively describes the gospel under the following headings: The Gospel is of God; The Gospel is Entirely of God; The Gospel is Entire in Itself; The Gospel is Preached; The Gospel Imparts Christ; and, Nothing But the Gospel Imparts Christ.

Price 25p *(postage extra)*
(Laminated Cover)
No. 1 in the Series

THE STRAIT GATE

'TRACT FOR THE TIMES' SERIES

The Strait Gate. Exceptionally well made, this booklet consists of extracts from 'The Messiah', compiled in such a way as to challenge the shallowness of much of today's 'easy-believism', whilst positively pointing to the strait gate.

Price 25p *(postage extra)*
(Laminated Cover)
No. 2 in the Series

ETERNAL SONSHIP
AND TAYLOR BRETHREN

'TRACT FOR THE TIMES' SERIES

Eternal Sonship and Taylor Brethren. This booklet is highly recommended, particularly for those perplexed by James Taylor's teaching against the eternal sonship of Christ.

Price 25p *(postage extra)*
(Laminated Cover)
No. 3 in the Series

MARKS OF THE
NEW TESTAMENT CHURCH
'TRACT FOR THE TIMES' SERIES

Marks of the New Testament Church. This exposition from Acts 2:42 declares what were, and what were not, the abiding marks of the church. The apostles' doctrine, fellowship and ordinances are lucidly explained.

Price 25p *(postage extra)*
(Laminated Cover)
No. 4 in the Series

THE CHARISMATIC DELUSION
'TRACT FOR THE TIMES' SERIES

The Charismatic Delusion. A prophetic message revealing the fundamental error of this movement which has swept away so many in the tide of its popularity. Here the delusion is dispelled.

Price 25p *(postage extra)*
(Laminated Cover)
No. 5 in the Series

PREMILLENNIALISM EXPOSED
'TRACT FOR THE TIMES' SERIES

Premillennialism Exposed. Well received evangelically, particularly through the influence of J.N. Darby, the Schofield bible, and the Plymouth Brethren, Premillennialism has assumed the cloak of orthodoxy. In this tract the cloak is removed, and the unorthodoxy of this system is exposed. A remarkable revelation.

Price 25p *(postage extra)*
(Laminated Cover)
No. 6 in the Series

JUSTIFICATION AND PEACE

'TRACT FOR THE TIMES' SERIES

Justification and Peace. This tract is taken from a message preached in December 1984 at Penang Hill, Malaysia. In this well-known address, peace with God is seen to be based upon nothing save justification by faith. No one should miss this tract.

Price 25p *(postage extra)*
(Laminated Cover)
No. 7 in the Series

FAITH OR PRESUMPTION?

'TRACT FOR THE TIMES' SERIES

Faith or presumption? The eighth tract in this vital series exposes the difference between faith and presumption, showing that faith is not of the law, neither is is apart from the work of God, nor is it of man. The work of God in man that precedes saving faith is opened generally and particularly, and the tract goes on to reveal positively the nature of saving faith. Belief and 'easy-believism' are contrasted, making clear the difference between the two, as the system of presumption—called easy-believism—is clearly shown, and the way of true belief pointed out with lucid clarity.

Price 25p *(postage extra)*
(Laminated Cover)
No. 8 in the Series

THE ELECT UNDECEIVED
'TRACT FOR THE TIMES' SERIES

The Elect undeceived, the ninth Tract for the Times, earnestly contends for 'the faith once delivered to the saints' in a way that is spiritually edifying, positive, and subject to the Lord Jesus Christ according to the scriptures.

The Tract is a response to the pamphlet 'Salvation and the Church' published jointly by the Catholic Truth Society and Church House Publishing, in which the Anglican and Roman Catholic Commissioners agree together about JUSTIFICATION. The pamphlet shows how they have agreed.

Price 25p *(postage extra)*
(Laminated Cover)
No. 9 in the Series

JUSTIFYING RIGHTEOUSNESS
'TRACT FOR THE TIMES' SERIES

Justifying Righteousness. Was it wrought by the law of Moses or by the blood of Christ? Written not in the language of dead theology but that of the living God, here is the vital and experimental doctrine of the new testament. Part of the book 'Justification by Faith', nevertheless this tract has a message in itself essential to those who would know and understand the truth.

Price 25p *(postage extra)*
(Laminated Cover)
No. 10 in the Series

RIGHTEOUSNESS IMPUTED

'TRACT FOR THE TIMES' SERIES

Righteousness Imputed. The truth of the gospel and the fallacy of tradition. Here the gospel trumpet of the jubilee is sounded in no uncertain terms, as on the one hand that truth essential to be believed for salvation is opened from holy scripture, and on the other the errors of Brethrenism are brought to light in a unique and enlightening way. This tract is taken from the book 'Justification by Faith', but in itself it conveys a message of great penetration and clarity.

Price 25p *(postage extra)*
(Laminated Cover)
No. 11 in the Series

THE GREAT DECEPTION

'TRACT FOR THE TIMES' SERIES

The Great Deception. The erosion of Justification by faith. All ministers, every Christian, and each assembly ought not only to possess but to read and reread this prophetic message as the word of the Lord to this generation, set in the context of the age. This tract is part of the book 'Justification by Faith' but contains within itself a message which is at once vital and authoritative.

Price 25p *(postage extra)*
(Laminated Cover)
No. 12 in the Series

A FAMINE IN THE LAND

'TRACT FOR THE TIMES' SERIES

A Famine in the Land. Taken from the Book of Ruth, with telling forcefulness this tract opens conditions exactly parallel to those of our own times. 'Behold, the days come, saith the Lord GOD, that I will send a famine in the land, not a famine of bread, nor a thirst for water, but of hearing the words of the LORD: and they shall wander from sea to sea, and from the north even to the east, they shall run to and fro to seek the word of the LORD, and shall not find it.'

Price 25p *(postage extra)*
(Laminated Cover)
No. 13 in the Series

BLOOD AND WATER

'TRACT FOR THE TIMES' SERIES

Blood and Water. Of the four gospels, only John reveals the truth that blood was shed at the cross. When it was shed, Jesus was dead already. With the blood there came forth water. But what do these things mean? With devastating present-day application, this tract tells you what they mean.

Price 25p *(postage extra)*
(Laminated Cover)
No. 14 in the Series

WOMEN BISHOPS?
'TRACT FOR THE TIMES' SERIES

Women Bishops? This is a question that has arisen in America, but should it have arisen at all?
Read this tract and find out the authoritative answer.

Price 25p *(postage extra)*
(Laminated Cover)
No. 15 in the Series

THE HEAVENLY VISION
'TRACT FOR THE TIMES' SERIES

The Heavenly Vision not only transformed the prophet himself, it became a savour of life unto life—or death unto death—to all the people.
'*Where there is no vision the people perish*', Proverbs 29:18. This is true. But where is the vision today? And what is the vision today? This tract answers those questions.

Price 25p *(Postage extra)*
(Laminated Cover)
No. 16 in the Series

EVANGELICAL TRACTS

EVANGELICAL TRACTS

1. **The Two Prayers of Elijah.** Green card cover, price 10p.

2. **Wounded for our Transgressions.** Gold card cover, price 10p.

3. **The Blood of Sprinkling.** Red card cover, price 10p.

4. **The Grace of God that brings Salvation.** Blue card cover, price 10p.

5. **The Name of Jesus.** Rose card cover, price 10p.

6. **The Ministry of the New Testament.** Purple card cover, price 10p.

7. **The Death of the Righteous** (*The closing days of J.B. Stoney*) by A.M.S. (his daughter). Ivory card cover, Price 10p.

8. **Repentance.** Sky blue card cover, price 10p.

9. **Legal Deceivers Exposed.** Crimson card cover, price 10p.

10. **Unconditional Salvation.** Green card cover, price 10p.

11. **Religious Merchandise.** Brown card cover, price 10p.

xlii

ECCLESIA TRACTS

ECCLESIA TRACTS

The Beginning of the Ecclesia by John Metcalfe. No. 1 in the Series, Sand grain cover, Price 10p.

Churches and the Church by J.N. Darby. Edited. No. 2 in the Series, Sand grain cover, Price 10p.

The Ministers of Christ by John Metcalfe. No. 3 in the Series, Sand grain cover, Price 10p.

The Inward Witness by George Fox. Edited. No. 4 in the Series, Sand grain cover, Price 10p.

The Notion of a Clergyman by J.N. Darby. Edited. No. 5 in the Series, Sand grain cover, Price 10p.

The Servant of the Lord by William Huntington. Edited and Abridged. No. 6 in the Series, Sand grain cover, Price 10p.

One Spirit by William Kelly. Edited. No. 7 in the Series, Sand grain cover, Price 10p.

The Funeral of Arminianism by William Huntington. Edited and Abridged. No. 8 in the Series, Sand grain cover, Price 10p.

One Body by William Kelly. Edited. No. 9 in the Series, Sand grain cover, Price 10p.

False Churches and True by John Metcalfe. No. 10 in the Series, Sand grain cover, Price 10p.

Separation from Evil by J.N. Darby. Edited. No. 11 in the Series, Sand grain cover, Price 10p.

The Remnant by J.B. Stoney. Edited. No. 12 in the Series, Sand grain cover, Price 10p.

The Arminian Skeleton by William Huntington. Edited and Abridged. No. 13 in the Series, Sand grain cover, Price 10p.

MINISTRY BY JOHN METCALFE

TAPE MINISTRY BY JOHN METCALFE
FROM ENGLAND AND THE FAR EAST
IS AVAILABLE.

In order to obtain this free recorded ministry, please send your blank cassette (C.90) and the cost of the return postage, including your name and address in block capitals, to the John Metcalfe Publishing Trust, Church Road, Tylers Green, Penn, Bucks, HP10 8LN. Tapelists are available on request.

Owing to the increased demand for the tape ministry, we are unable to supply more than two tapes per order, except in the case of meetings for the hearing of tapes, where a special arrangement can be made.

THE MINISTRY OF THE NEW TESTAMENT

The purpose of this substantial A4 gloss paper magazine is to provide spiritual and experimental ministry with sound doctrine which rightly and prophetically divides the Word of Truth.

Readers of our books will already know the high standards of our publications. They can be confident that these pages will maintain that quality, by giving access to enduring ministry from the past, much of which is derived from sources that are virtually unobtainable today, and publishing a living ministry from the present. Selected articles from the following writers have already been included:

ELI ASHDOWN · ABRAHAM BOOTH · JOHN BUNYAN · JOHN BURGON
JOHN CALVIN · DONALD CARGILL · JOHN CENNICK
J.N. DARBY · GEORGE FOX · JOHN FOXE · WILLIAM GADSBY
GREY HAZLERIGG · WILLIAM HUNTINGTON · WILLIAM KELLY
JOHN KENNEDY · JOHN KERSHAW · HANSERD KNOLLYS
JAMES LEWIS · MARTIN LUTHER · ROBERT MURRAY MCCHEYNE
JOHN METCALFE · ALEXANDER—SANDY—PEDEN · J.C. PHILPOT
J.K. POPHAM · JAMES RENWICK · J.B. STONEY · HENRY TANNER
ARTHUR TRIGGS · JOHN VINALL · JOHN WARBURTON
JOHN WELWOOD · GEORGE WHITEFIELD · J.A. WYLIE

Price £1.75 *(postage included)*
Issued Spring, Summer, Autumn, Winter.

Book Order Form

Please send to the address below:-

	Price	Quantity
A Question for Pope John Paul II	£1.25	......
Of God or Man?	£1.45	......
Noah and the Flood	£1.90	......
Divine Footsteps	£0.95	......
The Red Heifer	£0.75	......
The Wells of Salvation	£1.50	......
The Book of Ruth (Hardback edition)	£4.95	......
Divine Meditations of William Huntington	£2.35	......
Present-Day Conversions of the New Testament Kind	£2.25	......
Saving Faith	£2.25	......
Deliverance from the Law	£1.90	......
The Beatitudes	£1.90	......

Psalms, Hymns & Spiritual Songs (Hardback edition)

The Psalms of the Old Testament		£2.50	......
Spiritual Songs from the Gospels		£2.50	......
The Hymns of the New Testament		£2.50	......

'Apostolic Foundation of the Christian Church' series

Foundations Uncovered	Vol.I	£0.75	......
The Birth of Jesus Christ	Vol.II	£0.95	......
The Messiah	Vol.III	£2.45	......
The Son of God and Seed of David (Hardback edition)	Vol.IV	£6.95	......
Christ Crucified (Hardback edition)	Vol.V	£6.95	......
Justification by Faith (Hardback edition)	Vol.VI	£7.50	......
The Church: What is it? (Hardback edition)	Vol.VII	£7.75	......

Name and Address (in block capitals)

. . . .

. . . .

. . . .

If money is sent with order please allow for postage. Please address to:- The John Metcalfe Publishing Trust, Church Road, Tylers Green, Penn, Bucks, HP10 8LN.

li

Tract Order Form

Please send to the address below:-

		Price	Quantity
Evangelical Tracts			
The Two Prayers of Elijah		£0.10	......
Wounded for our Transgressions		£0.10	......
The Blood of Sprinkling		£0.10	......
The Grace of God that Brings Salvation		£0.10	......
The Name of Jesus		£0.10	......
The Ministry of the New Testament		£0.10	......
The Death of the Righteous by A.M.S.		£0.10	......
Repentance		£0.10	
Legal Deceivers Exposed		£0.10	......
Unconditional Salvation		£0.10	......
Religious Merchandise		£0.10	......
'Tract for the Times' series			
The Gospel of God	No.1	£0.25	......
The Strait Gate	No.2	£0.25	......
Eternal Sonship and Taylor Brethren	No.3	£0.25	......
Marks of the New Testament Church	No.4	£0.25	......
The Charismatic Delusion	No.5	£0.25	......
Premillennialism Exposed	No.6	£0.25	......
Justification and Peace	No.7	£0.25	......
Faith or presumption?	No.8	£0.25	......
The Elect undeceived	No.9	£0.25	......
Justifying Righteousness	No.10	£0.25	......
Righteousness Imputed	No.11	£0.25	......
The Great Deception	No.12	£0.25	......
A Famine in the Land	No.13	£0.25	......
Blood and Water	No.14	£0.25	......
Women Bishops?	No.15	£0.25	......
The Heavenly Vision	No.16	£0.25	......
Ecclesia Tracts			
The Beginning of the Ecclesia	No.1	£0.10	......
Churches and the Church (J.N.D.)	No.2	£0.10	......
The Ministers of Christ	No.3	£0.10	......
The Inward Witness (G.F.)	No.4	£0.10	......
The Notion of a Clergyman (J.N.D.)	No.5	£0.10	......
The Servant of the Lord (W.H.)	No.6	£0.10	......
One Spirit (W.K.)	No.7	£0.10	......
The Funeral of Arminianism (W.H.)	No.8	£0.10	......
One Body (W.K.)	No.9	£0.10	......
False Churches and True	No.10	£0.10	......
Separation from Evil (J.N.D.)	No.11	£0.10	......
The Remnant (J.B.S.)	No.12	£0.10	......
The Arminian Skeleton (W.H.)	No.13	£0.10	......

Name and Address (in block capitals)

. . . .

. . . .

. . . .

If money is sent with order please allow for postage. Please address to:- The
John Metcalfe Publishing Trust, Church Road, Tylers Green, Penn, Bucks, HP10 8LN.